W9-AJP-764

Off the map

THE JOURNALS OF LEWIS AND CLARK

EDITED BY
PETER AND CONNIE ROOP

ILLUSTRATIONS BY TIM TANNER

WALKER AND COMPANY NEW YORK

First published in the United States of America in 1993
by Walker Publishing Company, Inc.

Published simultaneously in Canada by Thomas Allen & Son
Canada, Limited, Markham, Ontario

Library of Congress Cataloging-in-Publication Data
Clark, William, 1770–1838.
    Off the map : the journals of Lewis and Clark / edited by Peter
and Connie Roop ; illustrations by Tim Tanner.
        p.   cm.
    Summary: A compilation of entries and excerpts from the journals
of William Clark and Meriwether Lewis, describing their historic
expedition.
    ISBN 0-8027-8207-8 (cloth)—ISBN 0-8027-8208-6 (lib. bdg.)
    1. Lewis and Clark Expedition (1804–1806)—Juvenile literature.
2. Clark, William, 1770–1838—Diaries—Juvenile literature.
3. Lewis, Meriwether, 1774–1809—Diaries—Juvenile literature.
[1. Lewis and Clark Expedition (1804–1806)   2. Lewis, Meriwether,
1774–1809—Diaries.   3. Clark, William, 1770–1838—Diaries.
4. Explorers—Diaries.   5. Diaries.]   I. Lewis, Meriwether,
1774–1809.   II. Roop, Peter.   III. Roop, Connie.   IV. Tanner, Tim,
ill.   V. Title.
F592.4   1993
917.804'2022—dc20   92-18340
                                               CIP
                                               AC

ISBN 0-8027-7546-2 (paperback)

Printed in Hong Kong

10   9   8   7   6

*For Rick, Nona, Chris, and Sara,
whose friendship has helped us
explore places off the map.*

PROLOGUE

In 1803 the United States purchased the Louisiana Territory from France for $15 million, or less than three cents an acre. This huge new addition, stretching north from the mouth of the Mississippi River to Canada and west from the Mississippi to the Rocky Mountains, doubled the size of the United States. President Thomas Jefferson decided to send an expedition up the Missouri River to map this region, meet with the numerous Indian tribes living there, examine the animals and plants, and find a route to the Pacific Ocean. Thus the stage was set for one of the most famous expeditions in American history.

Jefferson had carefully groomed Meriwether Lewis to lead this Corps of Discovery. Lewis, knowing he needed a dependable cocaptain, asked his old friend William Clark to accompany him. Clark gladly agreed and helped choose the 29 men needed to man the boats, men capable of enduring months of intensive labor and hardship. Tons of supplies necessary for a lengthy expedition into the unknown were selected: canned food, medicine, presents for the Indians, guns, bullets, scientific equipment, and hundreds of other items impossible to get in the wilderness.

So it was on May 14, 1804, that the three boats, manned by the "robust, healthy, hardy young men" of the Corps of Discovery, "proceeded on under a gentle breeze up the Missouri" and into history.

To record this momentous journey, President Jefferson requested that Lewis and Clark keep journals. Both men kept separate journals in the event one might be lost or destroyed. Many times, however, they combined their journal entries in an effort to save time and energy. When first published, *The Original Journals of the Lewis and Clark Expedition* ran to eight volumes, including one containing only maps.

This book, compiled from those journals, tells the story of the incredible journey of the Lewis and Clark expedition.

To Meriwether Lewis:

The object of your mission is to explore the Missouri River, as, by its course and communication with the waters of the Pacific Ocean, may offer the most direct and practicable water-communication across the continent for the purpose of commerce.

Beginning at the mouth of the Missouri, you will take observations of latitude and longitude, at all remarkable points on the river. Your observations are to be taken with great pains and accuracy. Several copies of these should be made at leisure times.

Objects worthy of notice will be: the soil and face of the country, the animals, the mineral productions of every kind, and the climate.

You will make yourself acquainted with the names of the [Indian] nations and their numbers; the extent of their possessions; their relations with other tribes or nations; their language and traditions.

In all your intercourse with natives, treat them in the most friendly and conciliatory manner which their own conduct will admit. If a superior force should be arrayed against your further passage, and inflexibly determined to arrest it, you must return. In the loss of yourselves we should also lose the information you will have acquired. To your own discretion, therefore, must be left the degree of danger you may risk, and the point at which you should decline; we wish you to err on the side of your safety, and to bring back your party safe.

To provide, on the accident of your death, and the consequent danger to your party, and total failure of the enterprise, you are authorized to name the person who shall succeed to the command on your decease.

Given under my hand at the City of Washington, this twentieth day of June, 1803.

Thomas Jefferson

President of the United States of America

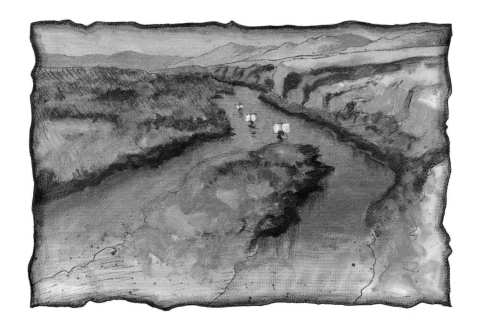

May 13, 1804. All our provisions, goods, and equipage are on board a boat of 22 oars, a large pirogue of 71 oars, a second pirogue of 6 oars, complete with sails, etc. Men completed with powder cartridges and 100 balls each, all in health and readiness to set out.

May 14, 1804. Set out at 4:00 P.M. and proceeded under a gentle breeze up the Missouri to the upper point of the first island, four miles.

May 15, 1804. The water here is very rapid, and the banks are falling in. We found that our boat was too heavily laden in the stern and she ran into logs three times today.

May 23, 1804. Set out early, ran on a log, and were detained one hour, proceeded the course of last night two miles to a creek. Captain Lewis near falling from pinnacles of rocks, 300 feet. He caught at 20.

June 16, 1804. Passed a prairie, covered with timothy, made our way through bad sandbars and a swift current. Mosquitoes and ticks are exceedingly troublesome.

June 27, 1804. We remained two days at the mouth of the Kansas River, during which we made the necessary observations and repaired the boat. On the banks of the Kansas reside the Indians of the same name, consisting of two villages and amounting to about 300 men.

July 4, 1804. The morning was announced by the discharge of one shot from our bow piece. Joseph Fields got bitten by a snake, and was quickly doctored with bark and gunpowder by Captain Lewis. We passed a creek 12 yards wide and this being the Fourth of July, the day of independence of the United States, we called it Fourth of July 1804 Creek.

July 7, 1804. The rapidity of the water obliged us to draw the boat along with ropes. We made 14 miles and halted. Saw a number of young swans. Killed a wolf. Another of our men had a stroke of the sun. He was bled, and took a preparation of niter, which relieved him considerably.

July 12, 1804. Tried a man for sleeping on his post, and inspected the arms, ammunition, etc. of the party. Found all complete. Took some lunar observations. Three deer killed today.

July 22–26, 1804. Our camp is by observation in latitude 41° 3' 11″. We stayed here several days, during which we dried our provisions, made new oars, and prepared our dispatches and maps of the country we had passed, for the President of the United States. The present season is that

in which the Indians go out on the prairies to hunt the buffalo. Five beaver caught near the camp, the flesh of which we made use of.

July 30, 1804. Walked a short distance. This prairie is covered with grass 10 or 12 inches in height. Soil is of good quality. The most beautiful prospect of the river, up and down, which we ever beheld.

August 1–2, 1804. We waited with much anxiety the return of our messenger to the Ottoes. Our apprehensions relieved by the arrival of a party of 14 Indians. We sent them some roasted meat, pork, flour, and meal. In return they made us a present of watermelons.

August 3, 1804. This morning the Indians, with their six chiefs, were all assembled under an awning formed with a

mainsail. A speech was made announcing to them the change in the government from French to American, our promise of protection, and advice as to their future conduct. All six chiefs replied to our speech, each in his turn, according to rank. They expressed their joy at the change of government, their hopes that we would recommend them to their Great Father (the President), that they might obtain trade. They wanted arms as well for hunting as for defense. We proceeded to distribute our presents. To the six chiefs we gave medals according to their rank. Each of these medals was accompanied by a present of paint, garters, and cloth ornaments of dress, a canister of powder, a bottle of whiskey, and a few presents to the whole, which appeared to make them perfectly satisfied. The air-gun was fired, and astonished them greatly. The incident just related induced us to give to this place the name of Council Bluffs; the situation of it is exceedingly favorable

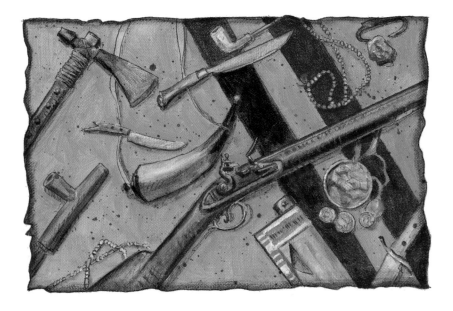

for a fort and trading factory. It is central to the chief resorts of the Indians. The ceremonies being concluded, we set sail in the afternoon. Mosquitoes very troublesome.

August 7, 1804. We dispatched four men back to the Ottoe village to apprehend one of the soldiers who left us under the pretense of recovering a knife and who we fear has deserted. The men had orders, that if Reed, the deserter, did not give up peaceably, to put him to death.

August 18, 1804. A fine morning. Indians arrived. We met with them near the boat, and gave them provisions to eat and proceeded to the trial of Reed. He confessed that he "deserted and stole a public rifle, shot pouch, powder, and ball." Requested we be as favorable with him as we could. We only sentenced him to run the gauntlet four times, and each man with nine switches should punish him, and for him in the future not be considered one of the party. The three principal chiefs petitioned for pardon of this man. After we explained the injury such men could do them by false representations, and explained the customs of our country, they were all satisfied with the sentence, and were witnesses to the punishment.

Captain Lewis's birthday. The evening was closed with an extra gill of whiskey, and a dance until eleven o'clock.

August 19, 1804. Sergeant Floyd is taken very bad all at once with a colic. He gets worse and we are much alarmed at his situation.

August 20, 1804. Sergeant Floyd died. Before his death he said, "I am going away—I want you to write me a letter." We buried him on the top of the bluff a half mile below a small river to which we gave his name. A cedar post with the name: Sergeant C. Floyd died here August 20, 1804, was fixed at the head of his grave. This man at all times gave us proof of his firmness and determined resolution to do service to his country, and honor to himself. After paying all honor to our deceased brother, we camped in the mouth of Floyd's River. A beautiful evening.

August 23, 1804. On the north is an extensive prairie which we called Buffalo Prairie for our having here killed our first buffalo.

August 25, 1804. We set the prairies on fire as signal for the Sioux to come to the river.

August 29, 1804. We had a violent storm of wind and rain last evening. Sergeant Pryor and his party arrived, attended by five chiefs and 70 men and boys. As a mark of great respect, they were presented with a fat dog, already cooked, of which they partook heartily and found it well flavored. The lodges of the Sioux are of a conical form, covered with buffalo robes painted with various figures and colors, with a hole in the top for the smoke to pass through. The lodges contain from 10 to 15 persons. The interior arrangement is compact and handsome.

August 30, 1804. Sent for the chiefs and warriors, whom we received at twelve o'clock, under a large oak tree, near which the flag of the United States was flying. Captain Lewis delivered a speech. We smoked the pipe of peace and the chiefs retired and they divided among one another the presents, smoked, ate, and held a council on the answer they were to make to us tomorrow. The young people exercised their bows and arrows in shooting at

marks for beads. The Sioux are a stout, bold-looking people. The warriors are very much decorated with paint, porcupine quills and feathers, large leggings, and moccasins—all with buffalo robes of different colors. The squaws wore petticoats and a white buffalo robe with the black hair turned back over their necks and shoulders. In the evening the whole party danced until a late hour. Their musical instruments were the drum and a little bag of buffalo-hide with pebbles in it and a bunch of hair tied to it. This produces a rattling music.

August 31, 1804. In the morning the chiefs sat down in a row, with pipes of peace highly ornamented. The grand chief spoke at some length, approving what we had said, and promising to follow our advice.

"I see before me," said he, "my Great Father's two sons. You see me and the rest of our chiefs and warriors. We are very poor. We have neither powder, nor ball, nor knives. Our women and children at the village have no clothes. I wish that as my brothers have given me a flag and a medal, they would give something to those poor people, or let them stop and trade with the first boat which comes up the river. I will bring the chiefs of the Pawnees and Mahas together and make peace between them. It is better that I should do it than my Great Father's sons, for they will listen to me more readily."

September 11, 1804. A cloudy morning. Set out very early. The river wide, and shallow, the bottom narrow, and the river crowded with sandbars. Saw a village of barking squirrels [prairie dogs], 970 yards long and 800 yards wide. These animals are numerous. Killed four, with a view to have their skins stuffed.

In the morning we observed a man riding horseback and were much pleased to find it was George Shannon, one of our party, for whose safety we had been very uneasy. Our two horses having strayed from us, he was sent to search for them. After he found them he attempted to join us, but seeing some other tracks, which must be those of Indians, and which he mistook for our own, he concluded that we were ahead, and had been for 16 days following the bank of the river ahead of us. During the first 4 days he exhausted his bullets, and was then nearly starved, being obliged to subsist for 12 days on a few grapes, and a rabbit, which he killed by making use of a hard piece of stick for a ball. One of his horses gave out and was left behind. The other he kept as a last resource for food. Despairing of overtaking us, he was returning down the river, in hopes of meeting some other boat, and was on the point of killing his horse for food, when he was so fortunate as to join us.

September 12, 1804. The day was dark and cloudy. We with great difficulty were enabled to struggle through the sandbars, the water being rapid and shallow so that we were several hours making a mile. We advanced only 4 miles in the whole day.

September 21, 1804. Between one and two o'clock the sergeant on guard alarmed us by crying that the sandbar on which we lay was sinking. We jumped up, and found that both above and below our camp, the sand was undermined and falling in fast. We scarcely got into the boats and pushed off, when the bank under which we had been lying fell in. We formed a second camp for the rest of the night.

September 23, 1804. Three boys swam the river and informed us that the band of Teton Sioux were camped nearby. We gave these boys tobacco to carry to their chiefs to tell them we would speak tomorrow.

September 25, 1804. A fair morning. All well. Met in council at twelve o'clock, and after smoking, agreeably to usual custom, Captain Lewis proceeded to deliver speech. All our party paraded. We invited the chiefs on board and showed them the boat, the air-gun, and such curiosities as we thought might amuse them.

Three of their young men seized the cable of the pirogue (in which we had presents). The chiefs' soldier (each chief has a soldier) hugged the mast, and the second chief was very insolent, both in words and gestures (pretended drunkenness and staggered up against Clark) declaring he should not go on, stating he had not received presents sufficient from us. Clark felt compelled to draw his sword, and made a signal to the boat to prepare for action. Captain Lewis ordered all under arms in the boat.

Most of the warriors appeared to have their bows strung, and took out their arrows from the quiver. As Clark, being surrounded, was not permitted to return. The pirogue returned with 12 of our determined men ready for any event. This caused the Indians to withdraw at a distance, leaving their chiefs and soldiers alone with Captain Clark. Their treatment of Captain Clark was very rough and justified roughness on his part. Captain Clark went back with his men on board the pirogue. He had not proceeded more than 10 paces before the first chief, third, and 2 Brave Men waded in after him. He took them on board.

We proceeded on and anchored off a willow island. Placed a guard on shore to protect the cooks and a guard in the boat. Fastened the pirogues to the boat. Called this Bad Humored Island as we were in a bad humor.

Wednesday, September 26, 1804. Set out early. Proceeded on, and came to; by the wish of the chiefs, to let their squaws and boys see the boat, and suffer them to treat us well. Great numbers of men, women, and children on the banks viewing us. They show great anxiety. Captain Lewis and five men went on shore with the chiefs, who appeared disposed to make up and be friendly.

Captain Clark was received on an elegant painted buffalo robe and taken to the village by six men and was not permitted to touch the ground until he was put down in the grand council house, on a white dressed robe. Soon after they set him down, the men went for Captain Lewis.

After a smoke had taken place and the chief made a short speech to his people, we were requested to take the meal, and they put before us the dog they had been

cooking, and pemmican, and ground potato. Pemmican is buffalo meat dried or jerked, pounded, and mixed with grease, raw. Dog, Sioux think a great dish, used on festivals. Clark ate little of dog. A large fire was made. Ten musicians played on tambourines, long sticks with deer and goats' hoofs tied so as to make a jungling noise, and many others of a similar kind. The women came forward, highly decorated, with the scalps and trophies of war of their fathers, husbands, and brothers and danced the War Dance, which they did with great cheerfulness, until about twelve o'clock, when we informed the chiefs that they must be fatigued amusing us.

October 10, 1804. A fine morning. We prepare to speak to the Indians. After the council was over, we shot the air-gun, which astonished them much. Those Indians were much astonished at Clark's servant [slave]. They never saw a black man before. All flocked around him and examined him from top to toe. He carried on the joke and made himself more terrible than we wished him to do.

October 26, 1804. We camped about one half mile below

the first Mandan town. Many men, women, and children flocked down to see us.

November 2, 1804. This morning at daylight Captain Clark went to look for a proper place to winter. Found a place well supplied with wood. Captain Lewis went to the Mandan village to hear what they had to say. In the evening returned with a present of 11 bushels of corn.

November 4, 1804. A fine morning. We continued to cut down trees and raise our houses. A Mr. Charbonneau, interpreter for the Gros Ventre nation, came to see us. This man wished to hire as an interpreter.

November 6, 1804. Last night late we were awakened by the sergeant of the guard to see a northern light. Many times it appeared in light streaks and at other times a great space light, and containing floating columns, which appeared to approach each other and retreat.

November 15, 1804. A cloudy morning. The ice runs much thicker than yesterday. The wind changeable. All hands work at their huts until one o'clock in the morning. Not one Indian came to our fort today.

November 16, 1804. A very white frost; all the trees all covered with ice. The men move into the huts, which are not finished.

December 7, 1804. A very cold day. The Big White, grand

chief of the first Mandan village, informed us that a large drove of buffalo was near, and his people were waiting for us to join them in a chase. Captain Lewis took 15 men and joined the Indians who were killing the buffalo, on horseback with arrows, which they did with great dexterity. His party killed 10 buffalo, 5 of which we got to the fort by the assistance of a horse, in addition to what the men packed on their backs. All the meat left out all night falls to the wolves, which are in great numbers. The river closed last night, ice 1½ inches thick. The thermometer stood this morning at 1 degree below zero. Three men frostbitten badly today.

December 19, 1804. The weather moderated a little. Captain Clark engaged in connecting the country [drawing his map of the Missouri].

December 25, Christmas, 1804. We were awakened before day by a discharge of three platoons from the party. The men merrily disposed. Some men went out to hunt, and the others to dancing and continued until nine o'clock at night when the frolic ended.

January 1, 1805. Fort Mandan on the N.E. Bank of the Missouri, 1,600 miles up. The day was ushered in by the discharge of two cannon. We suffered 16 men with their music to visit the first village for the purpose of dancing, by, as they said, the request of the chiefs of the village.

January 10, 1805. Last night excessively cold, the mercury at 40 below zero. Habits of the Indians have inured them to bear more cold than thought possible for man to endure.

February 11, 1805. This morning one of Charbonneau's wives [Sacagawea] was delivered of a fine boy.

March 29, 1805. Preparing to set out.

March 30, 1805. The ice came down in great quantities. The river rose 13 inches in the past 24 hours. Observed extraordinary dexterity of the Indians in jumping from one cake of ice to another, for the purpose of catching the buffalo as they float down.

For Mandan, April 7, 1805. Having on this day at 4:00 P.M. completed every arrangement necessary for our departure, we dismissed the barge and crew, with orders to return without loss of time to St. Louis. We gave Richard Warfinton the charge of the barge and confided to his care our dispatches to the government, letters to our private friends, and a number of articles to the President of the United States. (Male and female antelope, with their skeletons, 4 buffalo robes, 13 red fox skins, a robe representing a battle of the Sioux and Ricaras against the Minnetrees and Mandans. Cages containing living burrowing squirrels of the prairies, 4 living magpies, living hen of the prairie.)

Our vessels consisted of 6 small canoes and 2 large pirogues. This fleet, although not quite so respectable as that of Columbus or Captain Cook, was still viewed by us with much pleasure as those deservedly famed adventurers ever beheld theirs and with quite as much anxiety for their safety and preservation. We are now about to penetrate a country at least 2,000 miles in width, on which the foot of civilized man has never trod. The good or evil in store for us was for experiment yet to determine. These little vessels contained every article by which we expect to subsist or defend ourselves. The picture was a most pleasing one.

Captain Lewis esteems this moment of departure as among the most happy of his life. The party are in excellent health and spirits, zealously attached to the enterprise, and anxious to proceed. Not a whisper or murmur of discontent heard among them, but all act in unison and with the most perfect harmony.

April 13, 1805. We hoisted both sails in the white pirogue, which carried her at a pretty good gait until a sudden squall of wind struck us and turned the pirogue so much on the side as to alarm Charbonneau who was steering at the time. He threw the pirogue with her side to the wind, when the spritsail, jibbing, was as near oversetting the pirogue as it was possible to have missed. The wind abating for an instant, Drouilliard went to the helm and the sails were taken in, and the pirogue was again placed in a state of security.

This accident was very near costing us dearly. Believing this vessel to be the most steady and safe, we had embarked on board of it our instruments, papers, medicine, and the most valuable part of our presents for the Indians. We had also embarked three men who could not swim, and the squaw with the young child, all of whom would most probably have perished as the waves were high and the pirogue 200 yards from shore.

We saw many tracks of the white bear [grizzly] of enormous size. We have not yet seen one of these animals. The men, as well as ourselves, are anxious to meet some of these bear. The Indians give a very formidable account of the strength and ferocity of this animal, which they never dare to attack but in parties of six, eight, or ten persons and even then frequently defeated with the loss of one or more of their party.

April 26, 1805. Mouth of the Yellowstone. All in good health and much pleased at having arrived at this long-wished-for spot. In order to add to the general pleasure of our little community, ordered a dram to be issued to each person. This soon produced the fiddle, and they spent the evening with much hilarity, singing and dancing, and seemed as perfectly to forget their past toils as they appeared regardless of those to come!

April 29, 1805. We can scarcely cast our eyes in any direction without perceiving deer, elk, buffalo, or antelope.

May 5, 1805. Captain Clark and Drouilliard killed the largest bear we have yet seen. A most tremendous-looking animal, and extremely hard to kill. He had five balls through his lungs and five others in various parts. He swam more than half the distance across the river, and it was 20 minutes before he died. We had no means of weighing this monster. Captain Clark thought he would weigh 500 pounds.

May 17, 1805. Roused late at night and warned of the danger we were in from a large tree that had taken fire and which leaned over our lodge. A few minutes after, the top of the tree fell on the place the lodge had stood. Had we been later, we should have been crushed to atoms.

May 26, 1805. Captain Clark ascended the high country to view the mountains which he thought he saw yesterday. He beheld the Rocky Mountains for the first time, with certainty.

May 29, 1805. Last night we were all alarmed by a large buffalo that ran up the bank in full speed directly toward the fires, and was within 18 inches of the heads of some men who lay sleeping before the sentinel could make him change his course. He now took his direction toward our lodge, passing between four fires. Captain Lewis's dog saved us by causing him to change his course and was quickly out of sight, leaving us all in an uproar with our guns in our hands, inquiring of each other the cause of the alarm. We were happy to find no one hurt.

Today we passed the remains of a vast number of mangled carcasses of buffalo, which had been driven over a precipice of 120 feet by the Indians. They created a most horrid stench. In this manner, the Indians of the Missouri destroy vast herds of buffalo at a stroke.

May 31, 1805. The obstructions of rocky points and riffles still continue as yesterday. The men are compelled to be in the water even to their armpits, and the water is yet very cold. They are one-quarter of their time in the water. The banks and bluffs which they are obliged to pass are so slippery, and the mud so tenacious, that they are unable to wear their moccasins. Their labor is incredibly painful and great, yet those faithful fellows bear it without murmur.

June 3, 1805. This morning formed a camp on the junction of two large rivers. An interesting question was not to be determined: which of these rivers was the Missouri? To mistake the stream at this period of the season, and then be obliged to return and take the other stream, would not only lose us the whole of this season but would probably so dishearten the party that it might defeat the expedition.

June 13, 1805. My ears were saluted with the agreeable

sound of the fall of water and I saw the spray rising like a column of smoke. It soon began to make a roaring too tremendous to be mistaken for any cause short of the Great Falls of the Missouri. I hurried to gaze on this sublimely grand spectacle. I dispatched a man to inform Captain Clark and the party of my success in finding the falls, and settle in their minds all further doubts as to the Missouri.

My fare is really sumptous this evening: buffalo's humps and tongues, and marrowbones, fine trout, parched meal, pepper and salt, and a fine appetite. The last is not considered the least of the luxuries.

June 15, 1805. We set out at the usual time and proceeded on with great difficulty. We hear the falls this morning very distinctly. Great numbers of dangerous places. The fatigue is incredible: the men in the water from morning until night, hauling the cord and boats, walking on sharp rocks and round slippery stones. The rattlesnakes are innumerable.

June 16, 1805. The Indian woman extremely ill. This gave us some concern, as well for the poor object herself—then with a young child in her arms, as from her being our only dependence for a friendly negotiation with the Snake Indians for horses to assist in our portage from the Missouri to the Columbia River. Captain Lewis informed Captain Clark of his discoveries for our portage, and of its great length of not less than 16 miles. Good or bad, we must make the portage. We remain at this camp in order

to make celestial observations, restore the sick woman, and have all matters in a state of readiness to commence the portage.

June 22, 1805. This morning set out to pass the portage. Prickly pears extremely troublesome, sticking our feet through our moccasins.

June 24, 1805. The Indian woman is now perfectly recovered.

June 25, 1805. The winds are sometimes so strong in these plains that the men hoisted a sail in the canoe and it had driven her along on the wooden wheels. This is really sailing on dry land.

July 13, 1805. We eat an immensity of meat. It requires four deer, an elk and a deer, or one buffalo to supply us plentifully 24 hours. Meat now forms our food as we reserve our flour, meal, and corn as much as possible for the Rocky Mountains, which we are shortly to enter, and where, from the Indian account, game is not very abundant.

July 22, 1805. The Indian woman recognizes the country and assures us this is the river on which her relations live and that the Three Forks are at no great distance. This cheered the spirits of the party, who now begin to console themselves in anticipation of shortly seeing the head of the Missouri, yet unknown to the civilized world.

July 25, 1805. We proceeded on a few miles to the Three Forks of the Missouri.

July 28, 1805. Captain Clark was very sick all last night but feels somewhat better this morning. We called the south-west fork Jefferson's River, in honor of that illustrious personage. The middle fork we called Madison's River in honor of James Madison, and the southeast fork we called Gallatin's River, in honor of Albert Gallatin, Secretary of the Treasury.

August 17, 1805. Saw several Indians on horseback coming. The interpreter and squaw danced for the joyful sight, and she made signs that they were her nation. The meeting of these people was really affecting, particularly between

Sacagawea and an Indian woman who had been taken prisoner with her, and who had afterward escaped and rejoined her nation. The great chief Cameahwai proved to be Sacagawea's brother and is a man of influence, sense, easy and reserved manners. Everything astonished these people—the appearance of the men, their arms, the canoes, the clothing, my black servant, and the sagacity of Captain Lewis's dog.

Formed a canopy of one of our large sails for the Indians to sit under while we spoke to them. Through Labiche, Charbonneau, and Sacagawea, we communicated to them what had brought us into this distant part of the country. We wished them to collect as many horses as needed to transport our baggage to the Columbia. We made a number of inquiries about the Columbia River, the country, game, etc. The account they gave us was very unfavorable; the river abounded in immense falls, the mountains closed so close that it was impracticable to pass, that no deer, elk, or any game was to be found in that country. This information, if true, is alarming. Captain Clark to go in advance and examine the country.

August 18, 1805. At 10:00 A.M. Captain Clark departed with his detachment. This day I completed my thirty-first year and conceived that I had, in all human probability, now existed half the period I am to remain in this world. I reflected that I had as yet done but little, very little indeed, to further the happiness of the human race, or to advance the information of the succeeding generation. I viewed with regret the many hours I have spent in indolence. But

since they are passed and cannot be recalled, I dash from me the gloomy thought. In future, I will endeavor to live for *mankind* as I have heretofore lived for *myself*.

August 26, 1805. We collected our horses and set out at sunrise. We arrived at the extreme source of the Missouri. Here we halted for a few minutes. The men drank of the water and consoled themselves with the idea of having at length arrived at this long-wished-for point.

September 2, 1805. Set out early. Proceeded on through thickets, over rocky hillsides where our horses were in perpetual danger of slipping to their certain destruction. One horse crippled, two gave out.

September 3, 1805. At dusk it began to snow. Passed over immense hills, and some of the worst roads that ever horses passed.

September 18, 1805. Captain Clark set out this morning to go ahead with six hunters, there being no game in these mountains. This morning we finished the remainder of our last colt.

September 20, 1805. Proceeded on through a country as rugged as usual. Passed the head of several drains of a dividing ridge and descended the mountain to a level pine country.

September 27, 1805. All the men able to work commenced building five canoes. Captain Lewis very sick. Nearly all the men sick.

October 7, 1805. All the canoes in the water. We load and set out, after fixing all our poles, etc. Proceeded on, passing many bad rapids.

October 16, 1805. Determined to run the rapids. Proceeded on to the junction of this river and the Columbia. After we had our camp fixed and fires made, a chief came up from this river at the head of 200 men singing. They formed a half-circle around us and sang for some time.

November 7, 1805. Great joy in camp. We are in view of the ocean, this great Pacific Ocean, which we have been so long anxious to see, and the roaring made by the waves breaking on the rocky shores may be heard distinctly.

November 8, 1805. Proceeded on to a point. Waves so high

we landed, unloaded, and drew up our canoes. We are all wet and disagreeable.

December 3, 1805. Captain Clark marked on a large pine tree: "Capt. William Clark December 3d, 1805. By land. U. States in 1804–1805."

December 7, 1805. Ascended a creek 8 miles to a high point and camped. At this place we propose to build and pass the winter. The situation is in the center of, as we conceive, a hunting country.

December 12, 1805. Cutting logs and raising our winter cabins. The fleas were troublesome last night. We find great difficulty in getting these insects out of our robes and blankets. In the evening, two canoes of Clatsops visited us. These Indians appear well disposed.

December 25, 1805. Christmas. Awakened by the discharge of firearms and a salute, shouts, and a song which the whole party joined in under our windows. We would have spent this day in feasting, had we anything either to raise our spirits or even gratify our appetites. Our dinner consisted of poor elk—so much spoiled meat that we ate it through mere necessity—some spoiled pounded fish, and a few roots.

December 28, 1805. Directed five men to hunt. Directed three men to proceed to the ocean and make salt with five of the largest kettles.

December 30, 1805. Our fortification completed this evening.

January 1, 1806. Fort Clatsop. Awkened at an early hour by the discharge of a volley of small arms, which was fired by our party to usher in the New Year. Our repast, though better than Christmas, consisted principally in the anticipation of the first day of January 1807, when, in the bosom of our friends, we hope to participate in the mirth and hilarity of the day. Content with eating our boiled elk and wappato and solacing our thirst with our only beverage, *pure water.*

January 3, 1806. Our party, from necessity having been obliged to subsist some length of time on dogs, have now become extremely fond of their flesh. While we lived principally on the flesh of this animal, we were much more healthy, strong, and more fleshy than we had been since we left the buffalo country. Captain Lewis has become so reconciled to the dog that he would prefer it vastly to lean venison or elk.

January 5, 1806. The Indians gave us a considerable quantity of blubber of a whale which perished on the coast. We had part of it cooked and found it very palatable and tender. Resembles beaver in flavor.

February 14, 1806. Captain Clark completed a map of the country from the mouth of the Missouri to this place.

March 17, 1806. We have had our pirogues prepared for our departure and shall set out as soon as the weather will permit.

March 18, 1806. This morning we gave the chief Delashel-wilt a list of our names. Also pasted a copy in our room. The object of this list is that it may be known that the party who were sent by the United States in May 1804 to explore the interior of the continent of North America, did penetrate the same by way of the Missouri and Columbia rivers, to the Pacific Ocean where they arrived on November 14, 1805, and from whence they departed March 1806 on their return to the United States by the same route they came out.

March 23, 1806. At this place we had remained from December 7, 1805, to this day, and have lived as well as we had any right to expect, and we can say that we were never one day without three meals of some kind, notwithstanding rain, which has fallen almost constantly since November last. The rain ceased and at 1:00 P.M. we left Fort Clatsop on our homeward-bound journey.

EPILOGUE

The journey home was long and difficult. The expedition retraced its route back up the Columbia and then re-crossed the Bitterroot Mountains. In July they decided to split up. Lewis took one group to explore the Marias River, while Clark took the remainder to survey the Yellowstone. The two groups rejoined for the relatively easy float down the Missouri. On September 23, 1806, they reached St. Louis, where the entire town turned out to cheer the returning heroes who had been given up for lost.

The expedition had traveled over 8,000 miles on a journey that lasted two years and four months. Amazingly, Sergeant Floyd was the only casualty. His death was most likely due to appendicitis, something no one could have prevented at that time.

Lewis and Clark succeeded beyond anyone's expectations. Not only did they reach the Pacific Ocean, but they also mapped the interior of the Louisiana Purchase, made contact with the various Indian tribes, and collected invaluable information about the plants and animals of what would eventually become nine states. President Jefferson expressed "unspeakable joy" when he learned of the expedition's safe return.

Lewis and Clark were honored for their achievement. Lewis was made governor of the Louisiana Territory, a job he performed with limited success. Mysteriously, only three years after the end of the expedition, he died near

Nashville. No one is certain if Lewis killed himself in a fit of depression or if he was murdered. Clark became a much admired governor of the Missouri Territory, married twice, and had seven children. He died in St. Louis at age sixty-eight.

Soon after their return, Clark gave York his freedom and helped him set up a freight-hauling business. Sacagawea had died by 1828; no one is quite sure how or where. Her son, Jean Baptiste, lived to age eighty, serving as a scout and guide. Most of the other brave men of the Corps of Discovery have vanished from the pages of history. Several, however, enjoying the wilds of the West, returned to live among the Indians as trappers. Others became judges, businessmen, farmers, and traders. And, while their names are not as well remembered as Lewis and Clark, their bravery and endurance guaranteed the success of the Lewis and Clark expedition.

Glossary/Index

air-gun: a gun that uses air instead of gunpowder to fire a bullet. The expedition had one created especially for their use in case they ran out of gunpowder. The air-gun used by Lewis and Clark was almost as powerful as a rifle but made no noise or smoke. 10, 16, 18–19

ball: a round lead bullet about the size of a marble that was fired from a rifle. The men on the expedition made their own from lead obtained by melting down gunpowder canisters. 5, 11, 14–15, 25

barge: a flat-bottomed boat. Lewis designed one for the expedition that was 55 feet long and carried 12 tons of supplies. 23

bluff: a high bank or cliff along a river. 12, 27

buffalo/bison: a large, shaggy bovine with short horns. Huge herds of bison roamed the western plains of the United States. They were an important food source for the expedition. 8, 11, 13, 14, 17, 18, 21, 23, 26–28, 30, 36

Clatsop: See appendix. 35, 37

colic: a general pain in the stomach area. In the case of Sergeant Floyd it was most likely appendicitis, which no one at that time could have treated. 11

deserter: a soldier who leaves the military without permission; anyone who deserted the Corps of Discovery. Several of the men on the expedition, tired of the hardships encountered, deserted only to be punished when they were forced to return. 11

dram: a small amount of something to drink. Lewis and Clark used a dram to measure rations of whiskey. 25

equipage: the word Lewis and Clark used to describe all of the equipment/supplies they carried on the expedition. 5

garters: bands worn around the legs to hold up stockings. 10

gill: a unit of measure equal to 4 ounces or 1/4 pint. 11

Gros Ventre: See appendix. 20

jibbing: shifting a sail from one side of a boat to the other to keep the sail full of wind blowing from behind the boat. 24

latitude: the horizontal parallel lines on a map that depict distance north or south of the equator. 3, 7

longitude: the distance east or west of the prime meridian (an imaginary line running north to south through Greenwich, England). 3

Mahas: See appendix. 14

mainsail: the main sail of a boat or ship. 10

Mandan: See appendix. 20–23

mast: a pole used to hold up the main sail of a boat or ship. 16

meal: a coarse-ground grain such as cornmeal. 8, 28, 30

Minnetrees: Also known as the Gros Ventre tribe.

mouth: the end of a river where it empties into another river, a lake, or an ocean. 12, 15, 25, 26, 36–37

niter: also known as saltpeter, a key ingredient in making gunpowder. It was also used as an emergency medicine. 7

Ottoes: See appendix. 8, 11

Pawnee: See appendix. 14

pinnacles: jagged, pointed rocks. 6

pirogue: a type of canoe that can be sailed, rowed, or pulled. 5, 16, 23, 24, 36

platoon: a subdivision of a military company. 22

portage: to carry supplies and canoes around an obstacle such as a waterfall. 28, 29 powder: gunpowder. 10, 11, 14

prickly pear: a kind of flat cactus with sharp thorns. 29

Ricara: See appendix. 23

riffle: shallow water over rocks over which the expedition had difficulty dragging its pirogues and barge. 27

run the gauntlet: a form of punishment in which people were forced to run between two lines of men armed with sticks or weapons. Often used as a punishment for deserters on the expedition. 11

Sacagawea: the young Shoshone woman who served as a guide for Lewis and Clark from Fort Mandan to the Rocky Mountains. Her nickname was Janey. Desiring to see the sea, she carried her infant son Pomp all the way to the Pacific Ocean and back to her tribe. 23, 31

sandbars: mounds of sand in a river or lake. The expedition got stuck on or had to drag their pirogues and barge over numerous sandbars. 6, 14, 15

Sioux: See appendix. 12, 13, 14, 18, 23

Snake: See appendix. 28

spritsail: a sail extended by a pole. Used by the expedition to sail the pirogues and barge. 24

squaw: name used in the nineteenth century for a female Native American. 14, 17, 24, 30

stern: the back of a boat or canoe. 5

switches: long, thin sticks used like whips. 11

Teton Sioux: See appendix. 16

timothy: a tall prairie grass similar to hay. 6

wappato: a round, wild bulb like a small potato, which the expedition cooked and ate. Indians introduced this valuable food to Lewis and Clark. 35

APPENDIX OF NATIVE AMERICANS

Clatsop: This band of the Chinook tribe lived on the southern banks of the Columbia River. They built permanent wooden homes of split cedar. Their lodges were long and wide and had central fireplaces. The Clatsop lived in a wet environment with plentiful fish and wild game like elk. They used large canoes on both the Columbia River and the Pacific Ocean. The Clatsop were skillful traders and had first traded with Europeans in 1788.

Gros Ventre: This tribe called themselves the "Haamin," or "Men of White Clay." They were related to the Arapaho. This plains tribe were primarily nomadic hunters of bison. They lived in buffalo skin tipis that were moved to follow the buffalo herds. The Gros Ventre first traded with Europeans around 1754. Smallpox killed many members of the tribe in the 1780s. They were allies of the Blackfeet and enemies of the Sioux and Crow. Today many of the Gros Ventre tribe live in Montana.

Mahas: This tribe was the Omaha. Their name means "Those Who March Against the Wind." These plains Indians lived primarily west of the Missouri River in Nebraska and South Dakota. They farmed as well as hunted and fished. When the hunting season was on, they followed the game, leaving their villages behind. Their village homes were made of bark or sod supported by wooden frames. When hunting they lived in tipis. Lewis and Clark knew of the Omaha before the expedition began as their villages had been mapped in 1785. When Lewis and Clark reached them, they had just lost a major battle with their enemies, the Sioux. Today many Omaha live in Nebraska.

Mandan: This tribe called itself the "Numakaki," or "The People." They lived in permanent mound-shaped homes in North Dakota and along the banks of the Missouri River. Some Mandan villages had over 100 lodges. The Mandan were farmers, hunters, and traders. They had extensive fields in which they grew corn, squash, and sunflowers for food and trade. They fished the Missouri and other rivers, lakes, and streams. They hunted buffalo, deer, elk, and bear. The Mandan were in an ideal trading location as they were along the Missouri River and between the tribes of the southern and northern plains. Lewis and Clark spent their first winter near a Mandan village in North Dakota. They named their fort Fort Mandan in honor of these people. Smallpox nearly wiped out the Mandan in 1837, leaving only 128 survivors.

Minnetrees: *see* Gros Ventre.

Ottoes: Called the Otoes, this tribe lived much the way other plains tribes lived. They hunted, fished, and farmed. When game was plentiful, they left their villages to pursue it.

The Otoes were some of the first Native Americans Lewis and Clark met. Many Otoes now live in Oklahoma.

Pawnee: Their name means "horned," a reference to the way they wore their hair. They called themselves "Chahiksichahiks," or "The People." They lived primarily in Nebraska. Like many other plains tribes they were nomadic during the hunting season and lived in sod homes when not moving around. They farmed and fished as well. They were well known for their skills in making grass baskets and clay pottery. Their first encounter with Europeans was in 1541 when the Spanish explorer Coronado met them. Today many Pawnee live in Oklahoma.

Ricara: Known as the Arikara, their name came from the Pawnee word "ariki," or "horn" for the style of their hair. They called themselves the "Tannish," or "People." Like other plains tribes they hunted in season, but they also lived in permanent villages of sod huts surrounded by log walls. They grew corn and squash as well as other vegetables. This plains tribe rivaled the Mandan as traders. The Arikara today live in North Dakota.

Sioux: There were seven bands of Sioux people. The bands were the Santee, Nakota, Lakota, Dhegiha, Chiwere, Mandan, and Hidatsa. The name Sioux refers not to a tribe but to the language that these people spoke. Many Sioux live today in South Dakota, North Dakota, Minnesota, and Nebraska. Many also live in Canada. *See also* Mandan, Teton Sioux.

Snake: Better known as the Shoshone, this was Sacagawea's tribe. Lewis called them the "Sosonees," or "grass-house people." Sacagawea's band were primarily buffalo hunters. During the best hunting times they came down out of the mountains to hunt on the plains. During the rest of the year they lived in the mountains where they gathered wild foods like berries and roots. The mountain meadows also provided plentiful grass for horses. Sacagawea's band had many horses, which Lewis and Clark needed to cross the Rocky Mountains. The many Shoshone bands lived in a wide area ranging from Nevada to Wyoming. Many Shoshone still live in the western states.

Teton Sioux : The Teton Sioux were one of the seven major bands of the Sioux. They were also known as the Lakota and made up over half of the Sioux population. They roamed Wyoming, North and South Dakota, and Nebraska. The Teton Sioux had a reputation for being fierce fighters and were excellent horsemen. They lived in tipis and were nomadic, moving to follow the buffalo herds. They ate buffalo as well as other prairie game. Wild plants and berries supplemented their diet. They traded with farming tribes for corn, squash, and other vegetables. Lewis and Clark had their first conflict with a Native American tribe when some of the Teton Sioux tried to make the expedition pay to travel up the Missouri River. The conflict ended without bloodshed.